MW00965455

Healing Emotional Wounds

Those Deep Emotions
By
Grace Gayle

ISBN 9781973222750

**Biblical verses listed under WORKSHOPS are adapted and used for personalization of scripture by reader.

Contents

BOOK SYNOPSIS

Deep emotions are those which are imbedded in your character and may only be discerned by your closest friends or family. They are the ones that bother you when you are alone or trying to sleep. They prickle away at you causing you to feel less than enough of one attribute or too much of another.

- Have you ever been deeply wounded?
- Has someone betrayed your trust?
- Do you have difficulty believing God loves you even when you turn your back on Him?
- Are you over-sensitive or easily offended?
- Do you have trust issues?
- Does loneliness follow you?
- Is pleasing everyone all the time, top priority for you?
- Do you never seem to be comfortable in your own skin?

These struggles are symptoms of emotional wounds.

This book was designed to help you work-through the emotions and memories that keep you bound in your isolation. Its purpose is to help you find freedom.

INTRODUCTION

Confusion, loneliness, false guilt, shame, and worthlessness were never God's original design for you. These feelings are the aftermath of deep emotional wounds resulting from trauma. Heartbreak often opens the door for Satan to have a foothold in your life. These disturbing emotions are tools of the enemy of your soul.

You are destined for greater purposes. You were created to be the object of God's love. If you are a child of God, you are a new creation with a promising future. You can have victory over negative emotions.

When someone becomes a Christian,
he becomes a brand new person inside.
He is not the same anymore.
A new life has begun!
(2 Corinthians 5:17 TLB)

CHAPTER ONE
Confusion

In my anguish, I cried to the Lord,
and he answered by setting me free.
(Psalms 118:5)

Confusion feels like chaos in your mind. It attacks your greatest needs for, security, stability, and peace of mind. Your thoughts are cluttered, and you find it very difficult to make decisions. Your emotions are overwhelming as you overreact to situations you find yourself in. At times, you feel like you are a child in an adult body. You wonder if you are actually losing it.

Criticism and judgmental comments from friends and family add to your suffering. No one understands when you try to explain what is going on in your mind and emotions, so you pretend to be okay and try to act normal. But such behavior drives you further into alienation as you withdraw inside yourself.

Jesus understands your sorrow. No one understood Him either. He knows what you are feeling because He has been where you are. He not only took on the sins of every person who ever lived or will live; He took on the feelings of every negative emotion caused by the sins of others against you. Scripture tells us, *He carried our sorrows* (Isaiah 53:3-4).

From My Journal

I am told that one of the first steps to healing is to allow yourself to feel your real feelings. Yet some of my friends say, "Why are you digging up old memories and wounds? It's just making you feel worse. Stop feeling sorry for yourself. This will go on as long as you want it to. What's done is done. It's covered in the blood of Christ; put it behind you and move on in your life." But I can't!

Present experiences seem to tap into an immense reservoir of emotion, and I don't know how to stop it. When something upsets me, I don't just cry, I sob. I'm never in need of just a little affection, I feel like I'm going to die from loneliness. When something ticks me off, I'm not just a little angry; I fly into a fit of rage that erupts like a volcano looking to kill.

From My Journal

My counsellor tells me my confusion is caused from "feeling flashbacks or triggers." When more emotion is felt than what the circumstances call for, I am experiencing childhood emotions that were unable to be expressed when I was a child. Or they could be emotions from a previous wound that hasn't been dealt with.

Feeling flashbacks are somewhat like visual flashbacks, but you don't see anything happening. You have feelings, but you don't know what's causing them or where they're coming from. You go to bed at night feeling normal and, in the morning, you wake up severely depressed or angry or lonely. You can be going about your day when suddenly a powerful emotion comes over you. There's no explanation for it and you begin to think that you're going crazy.

Many times, I actually felt like a child. When I began connecting my intense emotions with childhood suffering, I realized I often felt the age I had been when that trauma took place.

After my counsellor explained "feeling flashbacks" to me, I would take some time when this happened and go to my Heavenly Father, asking Him to show me where the emotion was coming from. Usually it was something that had happened a day or two previously which triggered pain from past wounds. My Heavenly Father would take my memory back to where I had been wounded and comfort me while I expressed the appropriate emotion.

As my healing progressed, I felt like a child not as often. I noted that my feelings were maturing, and I was able to respond to difficult situations with adult emotions.

When I was a child, I talked like a child,
I thought like a child, I reasoned like a child.
When I became a man, I put away childish things.
(1 Corinthians 13:11)

FRIEND OR FOE?

How do friends help someone who is going through extreme emotional pain? Several people have said to me, "I felt so sorry for you when you were going through your depression, but I didn't know what to do or say." Others judged me mercilessly.

When I was at one of my lowest moments, I shared with Jenny about my suicidal feelings. I needed her prayer-support, and comfort, but she smugly told me that if I got my life right with the Lord, I would be okay. She could not understand how a person can be a Christian yet be so depressed that I would want to kill myself. Jenny's words went into my heart like a knife. I was trying so hard to cling to a God who had seemingly abandoned me. I needed a Christian friend to pray with me, to hold me, to encourage me. But all I got was judgment and rejection.

I found that my Christian friends had two differing opinions toward my depression. Some thought I was oppressed or maybe even demon possessed. Others beat me over the head with their Bibles, quoting scripture verses at me and telling me that the Lord never gives us more than we can bear. They would ask me if I was reading my Bible, implying that I must be a very weak Christian and wasn't walking with the Lord.

I wanted to tell them that I was not only reading my Bible at least two hours per day, but I was also studying and making notes, plus I was memorizing Scripture. I was also interacting with my verses as I talked with my Heavenly Father for at least one hour each day. *Did they think that was enough or should I double up on it?*

Scripture verses are very comforting, but they must be shared at just the right time, and from a heart that is filled with the compassion of a common experience. You must be sensitive to the Holy Spirit's leading.

From My Journal

Dear Jesus: I'm sorry if my faith is too small or if I'm drowning in self-pity. I don't mean to say that Your blood isn't strong enough to wipe away my wounds, but I hurt so much. I'm so confused. Why can't I put my wounds behind me? Please lead me in Your path for my healing.

"For I know the plans I have for you, [Grace]," declares the Lord, "plans to prosper you [Grace] and not to harm you; plans to give you hope and a future." (Jeremiah 29:11)

I am the Lord your God, who teaches you what is best for you, [Grace,] who directs you in the way you should go. (Isaiah 48:17)

I will lead [Grace] by ways [she has] not known, along unfamiliar paths I will guide [her]; I will turn the darkness into light before [her] and make the rough places smooth. These are the things I will do; I will not forsake [Grace]. (Isaiah 42:16)

One day when I got home from church, I said to my husband, "If one more person pats me on the arm and says, *'Just hold on to the Lord, dear. He'll never give you more than you are able to bear,'* I'm going to take off my shoe and pound her on the head until she cries out in pain and then I'll pat her on the arm and say, *'Just hold on to the Lord, dear. He'll never give you more than you are able to bear.'"*

David A. Seamands in his wonderful little book, "Healing for Damaged Emotions", comments on the needed area of healing:

"Through fifteen years, as tapes have gone out all over the world, letters and testimonies have confirmed my belief that there is another realm of problems which requires a special kind of prayer and a deeper

level of healing by the Spirit. Somewhere between our sins, on the one hand, and our sicknesses, on the other, lies and area the Scripture calls 'Infirmities'.

Understanding that Salvation does not give instant emotional health offers us an important insight into the doctrines of sanctification. It is impossible to know how Christian a person is, merely on the basis of his outward behavior. They're not fakes, phonies, or hypocrites. They are people, like you and me, with hurts and scars and wrong programming that interfere with their present behavior.

But, isn't it true that by their fruits you ye shall know them? (Matt. 7:16) Yes, but it is also true that by their roots you shall understand, and not judge them.

What I am saying is that certain areas of our lives need special healing by the Holy Spirit. Because they are not subject to ordinary prayer, discipline, and willpower, they need a special kind of understanding, and an unlearning of past wrong programming, and a relearning and reprogramming transformation by the renewal of our minds. And this is not done overnight by a crisis experience.

Understanding these things will protect us from two extremes. Some Christians see anything that wiggles as the devil. There is such a thing as demon possession. But only careful, prayerful, mature, Spirit-filled Christians should ever attempt anything in the nature of exorcism. I spend a lot of time in the counseling room, picking up the pieces of people who have been utterly disillusioned and devastated, because immature Christians tried to cast imaginary demons out of them.

The other extreme is an overly simplistic pat-answer syndrome, which says, "Read your Bible. Pray. Have more faith. If you were spiritually

OK you wouldn't have this hang up. You would never get depressed. You would never have any sexual compulsions or problems.

However, people who say such things are being very cruel. They are only piling more weights on a person who is in pain and unsuccessfully struggling with an emotionally rooted problem." [1]

Many times, I have thanked God for David A. Seamands and his book, *"Healing for Damaged Emotions"*. It has helped me tremendously in understanding that my struggles are rooted in my emotional scars and not in my walk with my Lord.

UP CLOSE AND PERSONAL

How to Be A Friend
Please, please, do not quote Scripture at the person of your concern, or ask if she is reading her Bible. This only implies that if she were more spiritual, she wouldn't have these problems. Possibly you could share a Scripture that has been a comfort to you but do it with gentleness and compassion. Give details of your own situation and how this verse has helped you.

Now, before you rush to pray for a compassionate heart that understands the depth of despair felt by an abuse victim, let me caution you. Compassionate hearts are grown, not given. They are earned through very painful experiences. However, I would challenge you to be willing to go through the pain necessary to grow a compassionate heart.

---

[1] Healing for Damaged Emotions, Selections from pg. 11-14, By David A. Seamands, Victor Books, A Division of Scripture Pres Publications Inc. U.S.A. Canada England

Genuine love and compassion go a long way in healing the wounds of a victim of any type of abuse. Her self-worth is so low that unconditional love is the only means of putting a bottom in her empty cup so that she can begin to fill up with love for herself.

She needs to learn that she can be loved without being abused, especially if her abuser was someone that she loved. If she has grown up in an abusive home, she will need someone to show her what God's unconditional love is like, since her view of her Heavenly Father will be distorted.

There's a neat little trick that I have learned that really works well in comforting a hurting individual. But you must ask her permission first as she may not be able to handle it at that moment.

You take your arms and wrap them around her upper back and pull her close to you. Hold her until you begin to feel her pull away from you. Then, release her and say something very simple like, "I love you," or, "I'm praying for you". Repeat this action as often as you see her.

You can do many practical things to help. You can clean her house. You can cook meals and take them to her home. You can take her out for coffee.

You can express your love for her by loving her children. They do not understand why Mommy cries all the time, or why she flies into fits of rage. Often, they blame themselves, resulting in painful emotional wounds which they will need to work through later in their adult lives.

Don't forget the husband. There is nothing that makes a man feel more helpless than watching his wife or children go through a severe illness or emotional pain which he can't control or understand. He too needs a shoulder to cry on; a listening ear that says, "I care".

Keep praying a hedge of protection around the family. Keep sending cards. Keep making phone calls. You can't do too much in showing your love and support.

Lend Me Your Hope

Lend me your hope for awhile,
I seem to have mislaid mine. Lost and hopeless feelings accompany me
daily, pain and confusion are my companions.
I know not where to turn; looking ahead to future times
does not bring forth images of renewed hope.
I see troubled times, pain-filled days, and more tragedy.

Lend me your hope for awhile,
I seem to have mislaid mine. Hold my hand and hug me; listen to all
my ramblings. Recovery seems so far distant.
The road to healing seems like a long and lonely one.

Lend me your hope for awhile,
I seem to have mislaid mine.
Stand by me; offer me your presence, your heart, and your love.
Acknowledge my pain; it is so real and ever present.
I am overwhelmed with sad and conflicting thoughts.

Lend me your hope for awhile;
a time will come when I will heal, and I will share my renewal,
hope, and love with others.
Author Unknown[2]

---

[2] Victory Over the Darkness, Pg. 14, By Neil T. Anderson, Regal Books, A Division of Gospel Light, Ventura, California, U.S.A.

You Knew the Anguish of My Soul

If only my anguish could be weighed
and all my misery be placed on the scales!
It would surely outweigh the sand of the seas.
No wonder my words have been impetuous.

I said, "I will watch my ways and keep my tongue from sin;
I will put a muzzle on my mouth."
But when I was silent and still, my anguish increased.
Therefore, I will not keep silent.
I will speak out in the anguish of my spirit,
I will complain in the bitterness of my soul.

Be merciful to me, Lord, for I am faint.
O Lord, heal me, for my bones are in agony.
My soul is in anguish. how long, O Lord, how long?
Turn, O Lord, and deliver me.
Save me because of your unfailing love.

In my anguish, I cried to the Lord,
and he answered by setting me free.
I will be glad and rejoice in your love,
for you saw my affliction and knew the anguish of my soul.
You have not handed me over to the enemy
but have set my feet in a spacious place.[3]

---

[3] Paraphrased from Job 6:2–3; Psalms 39:1–2; Job 7: 11; Psalms 6:2-4; Psalms 118:5; and Psalms 31:7–8.

CHAPTER TWO
Loneliness

In all their distress he too was distressed…
In his love and mercy he redeemed them;
he lifted them up and carried them.
(Isaiah 63:9)

A child watches as a mother cuddles her daughter in their play together. A teenage girl walks alone past a group of peers as they laugh together. A young man lays aside his values to become part of a crowd. A single mom flips the pages of a magazine as she watches couples strolling through the park. An elderly man picks a daisy and ponders the hole left in his heart by the loss of his dear wife. *Loneliness is a world-wide epidemic.*

Like a bottomless pit, once the emptiness takes hold it seems almost impossible to fill up with love. Like a leaky cup losing water; the hole in the sufferer's heart never seems to heal. No matter how many people reach out to help, love-hunger continues to gnaw away at the person whenever he or she is alone.

The best means of healing a lonely heart is developing a close relationship with your Heavenly Father. He knows how to fill all the cracks and crevices where loneliness lurks. He promises He will never leave you or abandon you.

The Making of Loneliness

I had been plagued all my life by loneliness. One day, I asked my Heavenly Father, *"Where does my loneliness come from?"* As I quieted my heart and allowed the Lord to comfort me through His word, He began to show me where my loneliness was rooted. He gave me a vision of a newborn baby lying with a bottle propped up on a pillow, signifying that this was how I was often feed.

During the first eighteen months of my life, our family went through four major crises. Three of my siblings became deathly ill with unrelated life-threatening illnesses. One was not expected to live more than two years, but she was miraculously healed and is still living today; the other two spent extensive time in Sick Kid's hospital in Toronto, but eventually recovered. The fourth crisis involved the teenage pregnancy of my eldest sister, who gave birth when she was only sixteen years of age. I'm sure my mother wanted to take good care of me, but she was just too weary and worn out to do the job well.

Loneliness has an opportunity to take root when a child isn't cuddled frequently. Often it promotes promiscuity when the child reaches his or her teen years.

People are created for relationship and physical affection, which is a very important part of interaction; however, we weren't a family that expressed physical affection. nor were we a family that shared deeply. Our emotions were hidden by humor; serious matters weren't discussed, at least not in a healthy way. Crises were not explained to the children, but instead treated as though they never happened.

We all wore masks to hide our loneliness and fear. We lived the empty way of life handed down to us from our forefathers. Consequently, I never bonded with my mother or any other member of my family except my one brother, who had recently died.

I don't remember ever being hugged by either of my parents. I'm sure it is because their parents never hugged them, either. You can't take blood from a stone. If it's not in you to give, how can you? *Physical affection—what is that?*

From the time, I conceived my first child, I prayed that God would teach me to be a good parent, and over the years the Lord has brought many people and circumstances into my life as a means of answering my prayers.

Lia, a Spanish woman who worked with me in the Ontario housing Ministry, began to reach out and pull me into a hug. I responded the way I always did to female affection… I stiffened. She said, "You're very cold, aren't you?" But she never gave up on me and gradually I began to warm to her affection. God also used a husband and wife doctor team who treated me throughout my healing process. They would hug me every time they saw me. They did much to teach me about healthy affection.

The third individual was Joanne, a newly converted prostitute whom I was discipling. She had been sending her two daughters to our Sunday School in the apartment building, and during a short time spent in jail for a misdemeanor, gave her life to the Lord. While I taught her how to walk in her new faith, she taught me how to first receive, and then give, affection.

The Scriptures give several examples of Jesus reaching out and touching people. Jesus touched the children. He washed the disciples' feet. He put mud on a blind man's eyes. Jesus often touched the people He healed, including the lepers whom nobody touched because they were considered contagious and unclean…

Years later, I picked up a book entitled *The Five Love Languages of Children*.[4] The book explains that there are five basic ways in which people are able to feel loved. Each person has one particular love language that speaks loudest to them.

The five love languages are:
- Physical Touch
- Words of Affirmation
- Quality Time

---

[4] Chapman, Gary and Ross Campbell. The Five Love Languages of Children (United Kingdom: Alpha, 1998).

- Gifts
- Acts of Service

As I read through this book, I began to see more reasons as to why I felt lonely and of no value. My love language had never been spoken to me as a child, and neither were any of the other love languages. But my Heavenly Father, in His love for me, brought people into my life who showed me physical affection, spoke life into me with their words of affirmation, spent one-on-one time with me, gave me little trinkets that showed they cared about me, and served me by providing practical help.

One day as I studied Luke 15:11-24, about the prodigal son, I noted that all these love languages were demonstrated by the Father.

When he came to his senses, he said… "I will set out and go back to my father and say to him: Father, I have sinned against heaven and against you. I am no longer worthy to be called your son; make me like one of your hired men." So he got up and went to his father. But while he was still a long way off, his father saw him and was filled with compassion for him; he ran to his son, threw his arms around him and kissed him. The son said to him, "Father, I have sinned against heaven and against you. I am no longer worthy to be called your son." But the father said to his servants, "Quick! Bring the best robe and put it on him. Put a ring on his finger and sandals on his feet. Bring the fattened calf and kill it. Let's have a feast and celebrate. For this son of mine was dead and is alive again; he was lost and is found." So they began to celebrate" (Luke 15:17–24).

- hysical Touch: "He ran to his son, threw his arms around him and kissed him" (Luke 15:20).
- Words of Affirmation: "This son of mine [he will not be a servant, he is my son]" (Luke 15:24).
- Quality Time: The son was to be seated in the position of honor, next to his father.

- Gifts: "Put a ring on his finger and sandals on his feet" (Luke 15:22).
- Acts of Service: "Bring the fattened calf and kill it. Let's have a feast and celebrate" (Luke 15:23).

My Heavenly Father speaks all five of the love languages to me. He is with me and comforts me in all my distress. He surrounds me with His love and calms my heart when I am afraid. He speaks words of acceptance to me and calls me His beloved daughter. He enjoys fellowship with me and enters into communion with me. He gives healing and restoration to my soul. He provides for all my needs—spiritually, emotionally, and physically.

The Lord your God is with you [Grace],
he is mighty to save.
He will take great delight in you [Grace],
he will quiet you with his love,
he will rejoice over you [Grace] with singing.
The sorrows for the appointed feasts
I will remove from you [Grace];
they are a burden and a reproach to you.
(Zephaniah 3:17–18)

God's Affection
Let the beloved of the Lord rest secure in him,
for he shields her all day long,
and the one the Lord loves
rests between his shoulders.

He tends his flock like a shepherd:
He gathers the lambs in his arms

and carries them close to his heart.

In all their distress he too was distressed...
In his love and mercy he redeemed them;
he lifted them up and carried them.

As a loving mother comforts her child,
so will I comfort you;
and you will be comforted.

I will take great delight in you.
I will quiet you with my love.
I will rejoice over you with singing.

In the desert the Lord your God carried you,
as a loving father carries his son, all the way you went
until you reached this place.

In a desert land he found you,
in a barren and howling waste.
He shielded you and cared for you;
He guarded you as the apple of his eye,
like an eagle that stirs up its nest
and hovers over its young,
that spreads its wings to catch them
and carries them on its pinions.

And he took the children in his arms,
put his hands on them and blessed them.[5]

---

[5] Paraphrased from Deuteronomy 33:12; Isaiah 40:11; Isaiah 63:9; Isaiah 66:13; Zephaniah 3:17; Deuteronomy 1:31; Deuteronomy 32:10-11; and Mark 10:16.

CHAPTER THREE

Guilt, False Guilt, and Shame

I trust in you; do not let me be put to shame,
nor let my enemies triumph over me.
(Psalms 25:2)

False guilt and shame can destroy a person. I struggled with both. The words "guilt" and "shame" are often used interchangeably but their meanings are quite different.

The synonyms for "guilt" are fault, blame, responsibility, and remorse. The synonyms for "shame" are disgrace, embarrassment, dishonor, and humiliation. Guilt is a condition of one's conscience, while shame is the state of one's self-worth. False guilt is the product of a warped or wounded conscience and is often rooted in shame.

A person suffering from guilt can confess their wrong-doing and be forgiven, but someone living with shame suffers from self-loathing and feels they deserve to be punished severely. An individual caught in the trap of false guilt will apologize over and over again and have difficulty accepting forgiveness.

From my Journal

My face turns beat red as I try to explain my feelings to my support group. I have such difficulty talking to more than three people at a time. Looking a person in the eyes makes me feel like they think I am guilty of something terrible. So, I drop my eyes.

Dear Jesus: If I am really forgiven and my sins are gone, why do I feel so guilty all the time? Why can't I hold my head up?

Once again, I turned to Scripture for my answers. The story of Jesus and the Samaritan woman, in John Chapter Four, shed some light on how I was feeling.

Around noon as he [Jesus] approached the village of Sychar, he came to Jacob's well... Jesus was tired from the long walk in the hot sun and sat wearily beside the well. Soon a Samaritan woman came to draw water, and Jesus asked her for a drink (John 4:5-7). (TLB)

The town's women normally gathered together early in the morning to walk to the well to draw water for the day. They made it a social time where they got caught up on each other's lives as well as the day's gossip.

So, why was this Samaritan woman arriving at the well during the hottest part of the day? And why was she alone?

As I read further down the chapter, I found my answers. After spending some time discussing spiritual issues, Jesus drew the woman's attention to what her need really was.

"Go and get your husband," Jesus told her. "But I'm not married," the woman replied. "All too true!" Jesus said. "For you have had five husbands, and you aren't even married to the man you're living with now." (John 4:16-18) (TLB)

Here was my answer. The Samaritan woman came to the well alone, in the middle of the day, to avoid the gossip, judgement and looks of disgust from the other woman. This woman was an outcast. Worse than that, she was considered the town's most immoral woman. She had gone from husband to husband and now she was living in sin with a man who was not her husband. She was disgraced.

The story doesn't give any background as to how this woman had ended up this way. Even in today's moral standards, five marriages would raise some eyebrows. But in that day, it was downright shameful.

This woman was guilt-ridden and carried the weight of disgrace of not measuring up. No doubt she also carried the shame of what others had done to her. Sadly, people are judged by their behavior rather than supported through the emotional wounds they have endured.

It was becoming clear to me that my issues where guilt and shame. I had to do some research to find out the difference.

Guilt says, "I have made a mistake". *Shame says*, "I am a mistake."

Guilt says, "I have done something wrong." *Shame says*, "What is wrong with me?"

Guilt says, "I can be forgiven." *Shame says*, "I am unforgivable."

Guilt is the convicting work of the Holy Spirit for the purpose of repentance. *Shame* produces self-loathing and is the chain Satan uses to keep his victim captive.

Guilt is God's unlimited invitation to leave your transgressions at the cross. *Shame* is the product of Satan's harassment, accusations, manipulation, and enslavement.

This is how Satan works in the lives of God's children. He tempts them mercilessly until they give in, and then harasses them ruthlessly with feelings of worthlessness and disgrace. His goal is to move his victims beyond guilt to the point of shame, so they become enslaved to him. A person who is wearing the cloak of shame will find it very difficult to get help since he thinks he doesn't deserve it; and he fears he will be judged and rejected.

Individuals trapped in a shame-based identity often struggle with false guilt. They feel guilty most of the time. If they think someone might blame them for something, they feel guilty. They feel guilty long after they have been forgiven and are unable to forgive themselves.

They often feel they need to pay pennants; as a result, they punish themselves harshly. They feel guilty when someone disapproves of their actions even if their actions are God honoring. They can't stand to have anyone disagree with them or be disappointed in them.

False guilt is self-abuse which keeps its victim on edge and living in fear of letting others down. They live on an endless treadmill of people-pleasing. These individuals are consumed with performance. They over-serve, over-give, and over-compliment, all to feel loved and accepted.

Shame is the consequence of taking on someone else's guilt or shame as in carrying shame for a parent who commits a crime and goes to jail, or for a sex-offender who blames his victim.

Children who have been abused sexually, physically, emotionally, or mentally often think they deserve the offence against them. They think that if they could just be smarter, prettier, better-behaved or different in some way, they would be lovable. Such children have very low self-worth and often marry abusive partners because they think this is what they deserve.

Once again, I am in awe of how my Heavenly Father protected me.

From my Journal

I am carrying disgrace for what was done to me. I am taking responsibility for shame that belongs to my abuser. I confess, I am guilty for how I have acted out in my pain, but I don't own what is his.

Dear Jesus: Thank You for carrying my guilt and shame to the cross. My sins and the sins of those who have abused me are paid in full. I will no longer carry shame that belongs to someone else. I will no longer pay pennants for what You have already paid for.

There is now no condemnation
for those who are in Christ Jesus.
Romans 8:1

Instead of your shame you will receive a double portion,
and instead of disgrace you will rejoice in your inheritance.
And so you will inherit a double portion…

and everlasting joy will be yours.
Isaiah 61:7

And you, because of my blood covenant with you,
I'll release your prisoners from their hopeless cells.
Come home, hope-filled prisoners!
This very day I'm declaring a double bonus—
everything you lost returned twice-over!
Zechariah 9:11-12 (The Message)

In you, LORD, I have taken refuge;
let me never be put to shame;
deliver me in your righteousness.
Psalms 31:1

Because the Sovereign LORD helps me,
I will not be disgraced.
Therefore, have I set my face like flint,
and I know I will not be put to shame.
He who vindicates me is near.
Who then will bring charges against me?
Let us face each other!
Who is my accuser? Let him confront me!
It is the Sovereign LORD who helps me.
Who will condemn me?
Isaiah 50:7-9

But in that coming day
no weapon turned against you will succeed.
You will silence every voice raised up to accuse you.
These benefits are enjoyed by the servants of the LORD;
their vindication will come from me.

I, the LORD, have spoken!
Isaiah 54:17 (NLT)

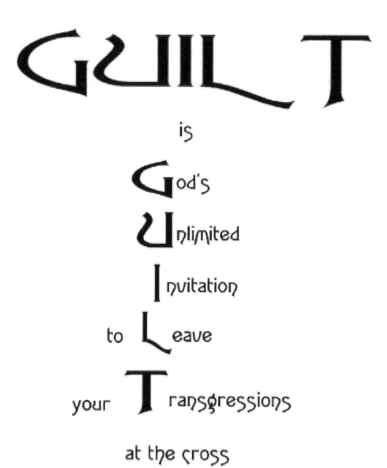

GUILT

is

God's

Unlimited

Invitation

to Leave

your Transgressions

at the cross

SHAME

is the product of:

Satan's

Harrassment

Accusations

Manipulation

& **E**nslavement

WORDS OF ENCOURAGEMENT

When you are feeling confused or lonely, take some time to review and meditate on the Scriptures in this book. Insert your name and roll the message over in your mind. Pray the words back to your Heavenly Father. Let yourself feel His love surrounding you. Thank Him for loving you and tell Him you love Him. As you allow the love of Jesus to wash over you, you will begin to see a difference in the level or depth of your painful emotions.

When you are attacked by your accuser through false guilt or shame, remind yourself and him that the blood of Jesus was shed for ALL your sins. There is now no condemnation for those who are forgiven.

So now there is no condemnation
for those who belong to Christ Jesus.
And because you belong to him,
the power of the life-giving Spirit has freed you
from the power of sin that leads to death.
Romans 8:1-2 (NLT)

Confusion, loneliness, false guilt, shame, and worthlessness are all deep painful emotions. We have talked about the first four emotions, but worthlessness will be discussed in my next booklet **"THOSE TURBULENT EMOTIONS"** because of the destructive way this emotion shows itself.

WORKSHOPS

Workshop One: Confusion

Confusion is frightening. You feel like you are walking on thin ice or a moving dock. Every step is uncertain, and unsteady. The path before you is a maze. Cry out to your Heavenly Father, He is always faithful.

Please reread **Chapter One: Confusion**

1. Please write out *Isaiah 42:16* on a card, inserting your name in place of the underlined words, adjust the grammar and memorize it this week.

I will lead the blind [confused]_____
by ways they have not known,
along unfamiliar paths I will guide them;
I will turn the darkness into light before them
and make the rough places smooth.
These are the things I will do;
I will not forsake them.
Isaiah 42:16(NIV)

2. What were some of the responses Grace Gayle received from friends regarding her illness?

_____

_____

_____

_____

_____

3. How do your friends respond to your situation?

_____

_____

_____

_____

4. How did Grace describe her confusion?

_____

_____

_____

_____

_____

5. How do you relate to Grace's experiences?

_____

_____

_____

_____

_____

6. How did God comfort Grace?

_____

_____

_____

_____

_____

7. How are you receiving comfort from God?

_____

_____

_____

_____

8. Please read the Scripture Collage, *"You Knew the Anguish of My Soul"* three times each day this week: Insert your name wherever possible.

Workshop Two: Loneliness

We were all created with a God shaped vacuum within our soul, longing to be filled with God Himself. If we don't fill this emptiness with God's love, we will be troubled by loneliness. Even individuals who received enough love and affection as children will experience a gnawing barrenness that drives them to search out new activities to fill the gap.

Please reread **Chapter Two: Loneliness**

1. What memories and emotions were stirred as you read the introduction of this chapter?

_____

_____

_____

_____

_____

2. Please write out *Zephaniah 3:16-18* on a card, inserting your name in the blanks. Read it aloud at least three times each day this week.

… "Cheer up, don't be afraid _____.

For the Lord your God has arrived to live among

you_____.

He is a mighty Savior. He will give you victory_____.

He will rejoice over you _____ with great gladness;

he will love you _____and not accuse you."

Is that a joyous choir I hear? No, it is the Lord himself

exulting over you in happy song.

"I have gathered your wounded[ness]

and taken away your reproach.

Zephaniah 3:16-18 (TLB)

3. What did Grace attribute her loneliness to?

_____

_____

_____

_____

_____

_____

4. How does your childhood experience compare to Grace's?

_____

_____

_____

_____

_____

_____

5. What are the five love languages of a child?

_____

_____

_____

_____

_____

_____

6. Which love languages did you miss out on in your early years?

_____

_____

_____

_____

_____

_____

7. Please read the Scripture Collage, "*God's Affection*" several times this week, inserting your name wherever possible.

_____

_____

_____

_____

_____

8. What emotions do you feel while reading this collage?

_____

_____

_____

_____

_____

9.   Write a prayer in your journal, asking your Heavenly Father to fill the hole in your heart.

_____

_____

_____

_____

_____

_____

Workshop Three: Guilt, False Guilt and Shame
Please reread Chapter Three**: Guilt, False Guilt, and Shame**

1.   What does Grace Gayle say her issues are in this chapter?

_____

_____

_____

_____

_____

_____

2.   Are you struggling with these concerns? Explain.

_____

_____

_____

_____

_____

_____

3.   Which Bible character does Grace identify with?

_____

_____

_____

_____

_____

_____

4. How do you relate to this woman?

_____

_____

_____

_____

_____

_____

5. What are you feeling as you read through this chapter?

_____

_____

_____

_____

_____

6. Please write out *Isaiah 1:18* on a card; insert your name in the blanks and read it three times each day this week.

Come, let's talk this over, says the Lord;
no matter how deep the stain of your sins, _____,
I can take it out and make you _____
as clean as freshly fallen snow.
Even if you _____ are stained as red as crimson,
I can make you _____ white as wool!
Isaiah 1:18 (TLB)

7. Describe the difference between guilt, false guilt, and shame.

_____

_____

_____

_____

_____

_____

8. What has Jesus done to take away your guilt, false guilt, and shame?

_____

_____

_____

_____

_____

_____

9. Write a prayer in your journal, expressing your thankfulness to Jesus.

_____

_____

_____

_____

_____

_____

W.A.R.R.R. WORKSHOP

1. If you haven't already done so, please write the verses from each lesson in your notepad for easier meditation.

2. Record in your journal the new insights you have learned about your W.A.R.R.R.

The Wound (how you were hurt)

The Affect (how the incident affected your life)

The Response (how you acted out your pain)

The Recovery (how your healing journey is progressing)

The Redemption (how your healing experience is changing you)

3. Please review all three lessons and write your thoughts in your journal.

ABOUT GRACE GAYLE

Chaplain: Fellowship of Evangelical Baptist Churches in Canada.

Founder/Director: "Healing Our Brokenness Ministries" (2014) the umbrella for her writing, speaking and life coaching.

Author: "*From Victim to Victor*" (2012)

Grace Gayle tells the story of her healing journey with transparency and straightforwardness.

"Healing Emotional Wounds" (2017), second addition of "From Victim to Victor"

"Healing Emotional Wounds Workbook" (2017)

Inspirational Speaker: The Healing Journey
    Personal and Spiritual Growth

Bible Teacher: Sharing practical help and encouragement from God's Word.

Freelance Writer: "*Healing from Dependencies*", Sage Magazine, Summer Edition (2015)

Grace has also written several leaflets on healing issues.

Creator/Facilitator: W.A.R.R.R Workshops

Grace lives with her husband, Paul McMullen, in Brighton, ON, and is a member of Evangel Pentecostal Church.

Contact Us:

www.healingourbrokenness.com
Email: gracegayle@cogeco.ca

Manufactured by Amazon.ca
Bolton, ON

34867933R00025